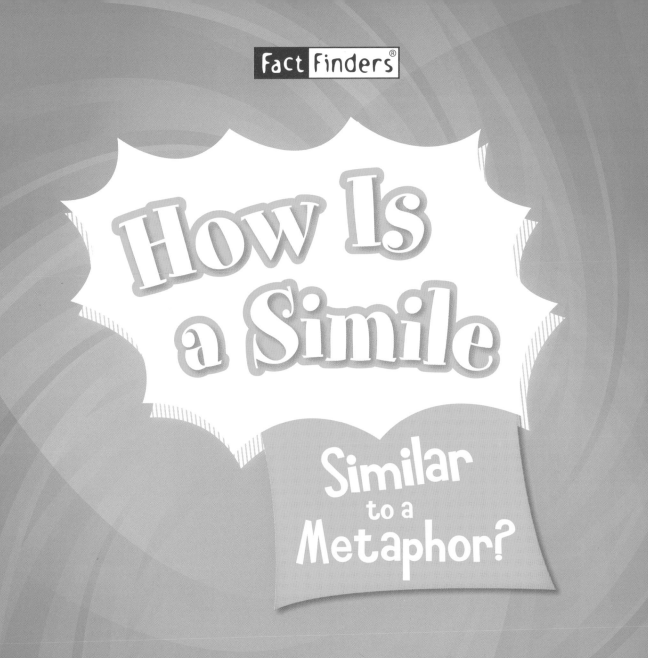

Fact Finders®

How Is a Simile a Simile

Similar to a Metaphor?

by Rebecca Stefoff

Consultant: Robert L. McConnell, PhD

CAPSTONE PRESS
a capstone imprint

Fact Finders Books are published by Capstone Press,
1710 Roe Crest Drive, North Mankato, Minnesota 56003
www.mycapstone.com

Library of Congress Cataloging-in-Publication Data
Cataloging-in-publication information is on file with the Library of Congress.
978-1-5157-6389-5 (library binding)
978-1-5157-6394-9 (paperback)
978-1-5157-6406-9 (ebook PDF)

Editorial Credits:
Michelle Bisson, editor; Bobbie Nuytten, designer; Tracy Cummins, media researcher;
Laura Manthe, production specialist

Photo Credits:
Alamy Stock Photo: David Shield, 8; Getty Images: Urbano Delvalle/The LIFE Images
Collection, 15; Shutterstock: 3DMaestro, 18, bom, 23 (bottom), Dmitriy Trubin, 21,
Elena Dijour, 22, Elvetica, 23 (top), Epsicons, 24 (bottom right), Eugene Onischenko,
19 (top), Everett Historical, 26 (bottom), Hong Vo, 17, Ilin Sergey, 24 (bottom middle),
Jennifer Stone, 20 (top), jgolby, 7, Kittikiti, 16 (bee illustration), kstudija, cover and
interior design element, Laslo Ludrovan, 4–5, lineartestpilot, 26 (top), littlew00dy, 28,
logistock, 24 (car emoji), Marish, 19 (bottom), matrioshka, 11, mhatzapa, 24 (mad face
emoji), MidoSemsem, 6, mixform design, 13, Morphart Creation, 25, Nattstudio, cover
(bottom left), photka, cover (bottom middle), rtbilder, 16 (bee photo), Skumer, 10,
Stephane Bidouze, 20 (bottom), Subbotina Anna, cover (right), Visual Generation, 12,
Vladvm, 24 (bottom left)

Printed in China.
010343F17

Table of Contents

CHAPTER ONE

Putting the
Wow in Words

Imagine picking up a new book and reading these lines:

> *The dragon had many long, sharp teeth. It glared at me with red eyes. It looked hungry.*

Now try a different book that starts this way:

> *The dragon's mouth looked like it was full of steak knives. The hungry glare in its red eyes said that I was all of its favorite foods rolled up into one bite.*

Which book would you keep reading? The facts are the same in both books. Some unlucky character is face-to-face with a hungry dragon. If you chose the second book, you probably picked it because the language seemed more lively and colorful.

In the second book, the writer used **figures of speech** called **simile** and **metaphor**. Writers use figures of speech to make their writing more pleasing or exciting. Similes and metaphors can also help a writer explain things, or make the meaning of a sentence clear and easy to remember.

figure of speech—a way to use words or phrases that goes beyond their actual meaning to create a colorful or striking effect

simile—a comparison that uses *like* or *as*, or a related word

metaphor—a comparison that shows that two things are alike by making it sound as if they are the same thing

Figures of Speech Are Everywhere

Writing can be divided into **poetry** and **prose**. Poetry includes poems, nursery rhymes, the words to songs, and some plays. Prose is everything that isn't poetry. Letters, essays for school, books, and stories—nearly all of these are written in prose.

poetry—writing that is arranged in lines that have a rhythm or beat and that often rhyme

prose—writing that is arranged in sentences and paragraphs

Poets and writers of plays have always used figures of speech. William Shakespeare wrote:

All the world's a stage,
And all the men and women merely players.

In this figure of speech, Shakespeare compared the world to a theater stage, and people to actors. What do you think he meant by that?

Young actors perform a Shakespeare play in an open-air theater.

Writers of prose use figures of speech too. In *The Hobbit*, J.R.R. Tolkien describes the home of Bilbo Baggins:

It had a perfectly round door like a porthole, painted green, with a shiny yellow brass knob in the exact middle. The door opened onto a tube-shaped hall like a tunnel . . .

By comparing Bilbo's front door to a porthole (a round window in a ship), Tolkien tells you that this is no ordinary house. When he adds that the hallway is like a tunnel, you may start to think that this is a place where anything can happen. (And it does.)

Stepping through a strange door is like entering a new universe.

Prose or Poetry?

POETRY	PROSE
Written in lines and verses (or stanzas)	Written in sentences and paragraphs
Has a pattern of rhythm or beat (also called meter)	Does not have a pattern of rhythm
Often rhymes, but not always	Does not rhyme
Usually has many figures of speech	Usually has fewer figures of speech than most poetry
May not follow punctuation rules	Usually uses correct punctuation

Stir in Something Extra

Writers are like cooks. They mix together words and sentences to create new dishes. Figures of speech are the spices and seasonings they use to add flavor.

Did you spot the figures of speech in that last paragraph? Writing isn't really cooking. Figures of speech aren't really salt and chili powder and cinnamon. If they were, these pages would be a mess. But comparing writing to cooking is a way of telling what figures of speech can do.

There are many kinds of figures of speech. In this book you'll meet three of the most powerful. They are simile, metaphor, and **personification**. You'll learn how to use them in your own writing— and how *not* to use them.

personification—a figure of speech that gives human features or abilities to an animal, object, force of nature, or idea

11

CHAPTER TWO

Like a Simile?

Teeth like steak knives. A door like a porthole.

What do those figures of speech share? They both compare one thing to another thing that is similar to it in some way. Those figures of speech are a special kind of comparison called a simile.

It's Similar

Simile and *similar* come from the same word in Latin, the language of ancient Rome. That word is *similis*, which means "like." Not as in "I like cake," but as in "That stale cake was like a cannonball with frosting."

Similes use *like* or *as* to say that something is similar to—or like—something else.

The baseball shot across the field like a rocket.
Aliens from Jupiter rode into town on beetles as big as buses.

Did You Know?

Every year there is a contest for people who try to write as badly as they can. One 2015 winner created this unforgettable simile: "The doctors all agreed the inside of Charlie's intestinal tract looked like some dark, dank subway system in a decaying inner city . . . however, to Timmy the Tapeworm this was home."

Not every simile has to use *like* or *as*. A simile can use *resembles*, which means "is like." Look for the two similes in this sentence:

> *The violin music resembled the screech of a thousand hyenas and seemed as long as an ice age.*

A simile can also use *than*. For example, Superman was said to be "Faster than a speeding bullet! More powerful than a locomotive!"

Invent your own similes and use them in sentences. Try to use *like*, *as*, and *than* at least once.

Good, Better, Best? Or Worst?

Writing that has no similes may also have no flavor. Too many similes, though, can get in the way of the story. Look at these three passages:

> All he could see was the figure of Riddle at the door, staring through the crack without moving. . . . Someone was creeping along the passage. He heard whoever it was pass the dungeon where he and Riddle were hidden. Riddle quietly edged through the door and followed.

> All he could see was the figure of Riddle at the door, staring through the crack, waiting like a statue. . . . Someone was creeping along the passage. He heard whoever it was pass the dungeon where he and Riddle were hidden. Riddle, quiet as a shadow, edged through the door and followed.

> It was as dark as a forest at midnight, so all he could see was the figure of Riddle at the door, staring through the crack as if he were peering at the moon through a telescope, waiting like a statue. . . . Someone was creeping along the passage as stealthily as a thief robbing a sleeping man. He heard whoever it was pass the dungeon where he and Riddle were hidden like two mice in a hole in the wall. Riddle, quiet as a shadow, edged through the door and followed like a guilty conscience.

If you thought the middle version was best, millions of readers would probably agree with you. It's from *Harry Potter and the Chamber of Secrets*. The first version has no similes. The third version has seven! In the middle version, author J.K. Rowling used two similes. She didn't overdo it.

TRY IT OUT!

Find some writing you like. Does it have similes? Try writing a version with no similes, or with too many of them.

When Similes Fall Flat—as a Pancake

As busy as a bee.
As hard as a rock.
Shaking like a leaf.
As fast as lightning.

These common expressions are not just similes. They are also **clichés**.

Not all clichés are similes. Any phrase or expression that is no longer fresh is a cliché. It may be easy to use, but it is also tired and limp, like a T-shirt that has been through the washing machine so many times that it's about to fall apart.

cliché—a phrase or expression that has been used many times and is familiar and stale

Because many clichés are similes, clichés may be the reason some people don't like similes. A writer named James Kilpatrick said that a simile is like the piece of parsley on a dinner plate in a restaurant. It's supposed to dress up the meal, but almost no one notices it.

When you want to spice up your writing, think of that sad little piece of parsley. Avoid similes that are clichés—such as *flat as a pancake*. Instead, use your imagination. The best similes are original, maybe even surprising. Above all, they are yours.

CHAPTER THREE

Metaphors—
The Magicians of Language

The great American writer Mark Twain once said, "Everyone is a moon, and has a dark side which he never shows to anybody."

Did Twain mean that every person is a small rocky globe circling a planet? Certainly not. When he said *Everyone is a moon,* he meant that there is more to people than we can see. Just as our moon has one side that always faces away from Earth, people have secrets and private thoughts that they keep hidden.

Twain made his point by using a figure of speech called a metaphor.

What's a Meta For?

Metaphor comes from two words in the Greek language, *meta* and *pherein*. They mean "beyond" and "to carry." A metaphor carries a word beyond its original meaning by saying that the word means something else.

Like a simile, a metaphor compares one thing to another thing. But unlike a simile, it doesn't use *like* or *as* to make the comparison. A metaphor simply says that one thing is another thing, the way Twain said that every person *is* a moon.

A metaphor is a kind of magician. With a wave of its word wand, it turns a person into a moon. When former president Barack Obama said, "Politics is a contact sport," his metaphor turned politics into a rough-and-tumble sport such as football. It made the point that politics can be rough too.

If one of your friends says, "On weekends my mom is a crazy cleaning robot," do you worry that your friend's mother regularly turns into an insane metal janitor? No. You know that your friend meant, "My mother does a *lot* of housecleaning on weekends." The metaphor made a stronger point.

When Metaphors Go Wrong

Metaphors can add power and beauty to what you write or say. But bad metaphors can leave readers scratching their heads in puzzlement, saying, "Huh?"

Some bad metaphors just don't say anything useful. Suppose you are reading a story about a painter and you come across this sentence: *Art is a lonely marble.* It's a metaphor, but what does it mean? If the meaning isn't clear, the metaphor isn't doing its job.

Mixed metaphors are just as bad. They happen when a writer starts with a metaphor, then throws in another one that doesn't fit in with the first one.

In a story about bankers, novelist Tom Wolfe wrote, "All at once he was alone in this noisy hive with no place to roost." Even if you know what he meant, the metaphor feels weird. It compares a place to a hive (where bees live) but then says there's nowhere to roost (something that birds do).

An Irish politician once said, "I smell a rat. I see him floating in the air. But . . . I will nip him in the bud." This metaphor mixes the smell of a rat (something dishonest or tricky) with the image of a flying rat (what!?). It ends with a gardening term that means to cut something off before it can grow.

Watch out for mixed metaphors. They can go horribly wrong, like Frankenstein's monster smashing buildings in Tokyo.

Making a Metaphor Longer

Many metaphors are short and sweet. They say one thing and make their point. *Music is food for the heart* is that kind of metaphor.

Other metaphors are longer because they have more than one part. A long metaphor with more than one part is called an extended metaphor.

Here's an extended metaphor from the famous scientist Albert Einstein:

> *Life is a great tapestry. The individual is only an insignificant thread in an immense and miraculous pattern.*

Einstein's basic metaphor is that life is a tapestry, which is a picture woven into a large cloth. To keep the metaphor going, he says that each person is a thread in the tapestry. He ties the metaphor together by saying that all the threads make up a pattern.

Once you have your basic metaphor, see if you can find ways to keep it going:

That book is a house with many rooms. Each time I read it, I open a door and discover a new one. Sometimes it's a bathroom, sometimes it's a bedroom.

TRY IT OUT!

Try making up an extended metaphor. One way to start is to think of something you like, such as a favorite book or movie. What can you compare it to? A roller-coaster ride? A warm bath? A party with friends?

New Tools and New Metaphors

MAKING METAPHORS BY EMOJI

My room is

I'll bet your mom is

METAPHORS FOR THE INTERNET

World Wide Web

Information Superhighway

The Cloud

CHAPTER FOUR

The Power of Personification

A girl named Alice meets a talking rabbit in the book *Alice's Adventures in Wonderland*. That rabbit doesn't just talk. He carries a pocket watch, wears a jacket, and worries about being late to a party. In short, he acts a lot like a person.

The White Rabbit in Alice's story is an example of a special kind of metaphor called personification.

Becoming Human

Personification turns something that isn't human into something that has at least one human feature. The nonhuman thing can be an animal, an object, a force of nature, or even an idea.

Here are some examples of personification:

The frog said to the princess, "Kiss me! I'm really a prince."
(animal/frog)

Box Trolls tell the funniest jokes.
(object/cardboard boxes)

The sun smiled down on the morning meadow.
(force of nature/sun)

The Statue of Liberty welcomes people to America's shores.
(idea/freedom)

Storytellers have used personification for thousands of years. The ancient Greek stories known as *Aesop's Fables* are just one example. They are full of animals and objects that talk and act like people—usually to teach people a lesson of some kind.

You may have seen personification in cartoons, movies, or video games. Talking cars, toys, and fish are examples. So are made-up "people" who stand for things that can't be seen, such as Uncle Sam. He is an old man dressed in red, white, and blue who stands for the U.S. government.

Did You Know?

The personification of the U.S. government as "Uncle Sam" started more than 200 years ago, during the War of 1812. The best-known picture of him as a white-whiskered old man came into being a hundred years later. The government used it on a poster to urge young men to join the army during World War I (1914–1918).

I WANT YOU FOR U.S. ARMY
NEAREST RECRUITING STATION

Know Your Figures of Speech

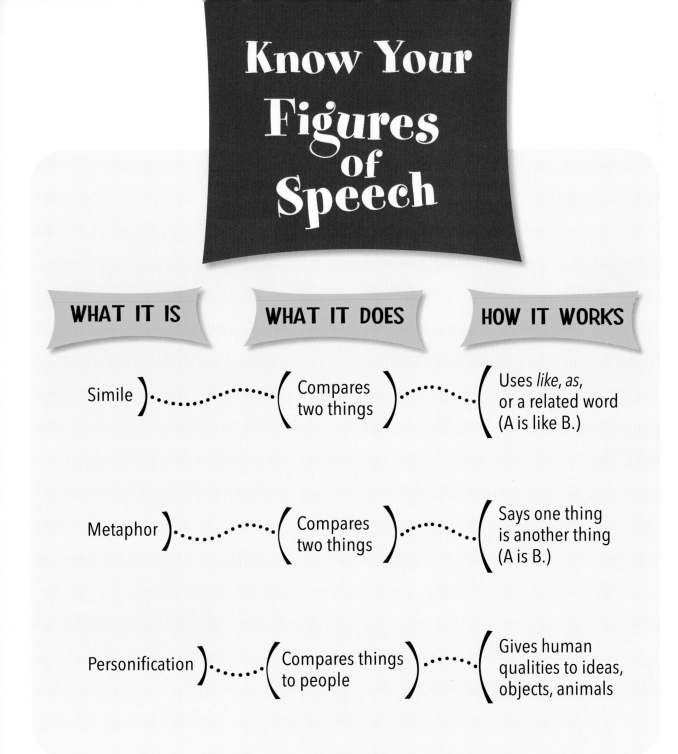

WHAT IT IS	WHAT IT DOES	HOW IT WORKS
Simile	Compares two things	Uses *like, as*, or a related word (A is like B.)
Metaphor	Compares two things	Says one thing is another thing (A is B.)
Personification	Compares things to people	Gives human qualities to ideas, objects, animals

Why Personify?

Writers use personification for three reasons.

One   It's entertaining. Many people—especially young people—think it's fun to read about animals and things that act like people. Fairy tales, fantasy and adventure stories, and games use personification to create a world that is different from the everyday world.

Two   It can create strong feelings in readers. If you were writing a scary story, would you say, "The wind blew the dry branches against the window"? Or would you personify those branches and say, "The dry branches tapped and clawed at the glass"? The second version makes it feel as if the trees were trying to get inside. Creepy!

Three   It lets writers make a point or teach a lesson. *Aesop's Fables* "The Dog in the Manger" is a good example. A dog refuses to let a cow or horse eat some grain, even though the dog can't eat grain and has no use for it. The fable uses animals to show how some people are mean enough to hurt others even when doing so does them no good.

TRY IT OUT!

Add personification to your writing tool kit, along with simile and metaphor. Maybe you'll be the one to write the next great talking-animal story!

Simile, Metaphor, or Personification?

Can you tell whether each of these figures of speech
is a simile, metaphor, or personification?

 Those cookies were begging me to eat them!

 "Writing, to me, is simply thinking through my fingers."
(science fiction writer Isaac Asimov)

 "The woods are getting ready to sleep . . . " (from *The Green Gables Letters,* by L.M. Montgomery)

 The ghost's hands moved like a pair of big, pale spiders.

 School is a long row of hills. You spend all year climbing to get up and over one grade. The other side is a valley where you can play for the summer, but after that, you start climbing the next hill. Each hill is a little harder to climb, but at the top of each one, you can see farther than before.

 "And when their voices faded away, it was as quiet as a dream." (from *Owl Moon,* by Jane Yolen)

[See answers on page 31.]

Glossary

cliché (klee-SHAY)—a phrase or expression that has been used many times and is familiar and stale

figure of speech (fi-GUYR-uvv-speech)—a way to use words or phrases that goes beyond their actual meaning to create a colorful or striking effect

metaphor (meht-uh-FOR)—a comparison that shows that two things are alike by making it sound as if they are the same thing

personification (per-sa-ne-fuh-CA-shun)—a figure of speech that gives human features or abilities to an animal, object, force of nature, or idea

poetry (po-eh-TREE)—writing that is arranged in lines that have a rhythm or beat and that often rhyme

prose (PROHZ)—writing that is arranged in sentences and paragraphs.

simile (SIM-uh-lee)—a figure of speech that uses like or as, or a related word

Read More

Heinrichs, Ann. *Similes and Metaphors.* North Mankato, Minn: Child's World, 2014.

Johnson, Robin. *Understanding Metaphors.* Figuratively Speaking. New York: Crabtree Publishing Company, 2016.

Murray, Kara. *Similes and Metaphors.* New York: PowerKids Press, 2015.

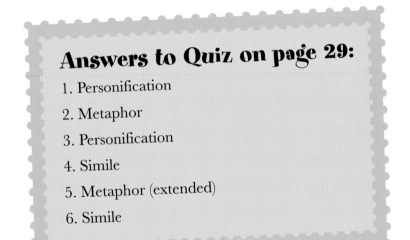

Answers to Quiz on page 29:

1. Personification

2. Metaphor

3. Personification

4. Simile

5. Metaphor (extended)

6. Simile

Critical Thinking Questions

1. The title of this book is *How Is a Simile Like a Metaphor?* Write down how similes and metaphors are alike. Now write about how they are different. What is the main difference? Give examples of similes and metaphors from the text.

2. List as many similes as you can. Start with some of the ones in this book. Now look closely at them. Are any of them clichés or familiar phrases such as *flat as a pancake?* If they are, create new similes to use instead, for example, *flat as a brand-new sidewalk.*

3. Write a paragraph about an animal, using similes and metaphors. Then write a new paragraph about the same animal, this time using personification. Do you like one version more than the other? Why or why not?

Internet Sites

Use FactHound to find Internet sites related to this book.

Visit *www.facthound.com*

Just type in 9781515763895 and go.

 Check out projects, games and lots more at
www.capstonekids.com

Index